LITTLE BOOK OF

CATS

LITTLE BOOK OF
CATS

First published in the UK in 2008

© G2 Entertainment Limited 2014

www.G2ent.co.uk

Printed and bound in Europe

ISBN 978-1-782812-59-3

Contents

Introduction

Thousands of years ago the humble cat was worshipped as a god. This is a fact that, even today, cats enjoy reminding us of on a regular basis. And they have plenty of people to remind; in the United Kingdom alone over eight million felines are kept as pets whilst in the United States an incredible 70 million purrfect companions grace the homes of cat aficionados from New York to New Mexico.

Some would argue that you never actually own a cat but that you are merely the human with whom it chooses to spend its time. Others, usually those who buy its food and pay for its veterinary bills, might have another opinion. All, however, would agree that a feline friend is pretty hard to beat. But why own (or be owned by) a cat?

Whilst, for some people, certain breeds might stretch the limits of aesthetic acceptability, it is generally acknowledged that cats are elegant, graceful and rather beautiful to look at. What better accessory for the perfectly decorated home than a perfectly designed feline?

Cats offer wonderful companionship. What better way to end a hard day's work than to return home and be greeted by a loving feline friend or to be accompanied by one throughout the day if you are housebound?

Cats are (generally) low maintenance. Obviously regular grooming and a healthy diet are an absolute must but, whilst dogs require countless walks come rain, shine, snow or sleet, the average cat will be quite

happy curled up in a ball on the sofa, on the bed, on your favourite chair or, most importantly, on your lap.

There are, however, more tangible reasons for bringing a cat into your life. In 2008, the results of a study conducted by Professor Qureshi of the University of Minnesota revealed that owning a cat could reduce the risk of heart attacks and strokes by as much as

a third by relieving stress and anxiety and subsequently reducing the risk of heart disease. Perhaps British Shorthairs and Japanese Bobtails should be available on prescription?

Whatever the reasons, there can be little doubt that owning a cat can bring something a little special into anybody's life… and the cats seem to approve of it too!

A Cat's Life –
A Brief History Of Purring

Early Domestication

Despite what Messrs Hanna and Barbera would have had you believe, the first example of man's long term affinity with the feline species did not involve putting the sabre tooth tiger out with the milk bottles at the end of a hard day's work at the stone quarry.

It is common thinking that cats of one sort or another have stalked the earth for the best part of 12 million years, but it was not until at least the twentieth or nineteenth century BC that they were first tamed and bred by mankind. 10,000-year-old carvings and pottery dating to the Neolithic (late Stone Age) period have been found which contain images of cats and, more recently, the carefully interred 9,500-year-old remains of a human and a cat were found in a grave at Shillourokambos on the Mediterranean island of Cyprus providing evidence that, even then, felines were considered to possess at least a spiritual significance.

Probably the most significant evidence of early domestication heralds from ancient Egypt and the time of the Pharaohs where cats were not only employed as guardians of the valuable grain stores but were also worshipped as deities with the goddesses Sekhmet (the god of war) and Bastet (the god of protection) often being represented in feline form. Such was their place in society, when a cat died it was often mummified before being taken to be laid to rest in the temple at Bubastis. A large number of these mummies have survived to this day allowing scientists to identify this early domestic species as a derivative of *Felis libyca*, the African Wild Cat.

In around 900BC the first Egyptian cats started to arrive in Italy aboard the ships of Phoenician traders from where they gradually spread across Europe before finally reaching British shores in the early Middle Ages where they were seen as a rare curiosity and soon formed the basis of many tales of folklore and superstition.

During the sixteenth century the first of the longhair breeds started to be seen in Europe having arrived from Turkey, Persia and regions that are now part of Afghanistan. These cats, in turn, may themselves have developed over time from the O*tocolobus manul,* the beautiful longhaired wild Pallas' Cat, or manul, of the Central Asian steppes – a breed once hunted in enormous numbers for its fur by Mongolian tribesmen almost to the point of extinction.

Whilst a substantially different affair from what we would recognise today, the world's first cat show is thought to have taken place in 1598 as part of St Giles' Fair in Winchester, England. However, in these early years breed standards, correct confirmation and perfect colouring were not on the agenda – a cat's worth being judged far

Altägyptiſche Katzen=Mumien von Bubaſtis und Beni=Haſan
Originale in der Landwirtſchaftlichen Sammlung, Zürich

LITTLE BOOK OF **CATS**

more by its mousing ability!

The first cats to reach North American shores did so in the sixteenth century. Accompanying the early settlers on their travels, they earned their keep aboard ship as experts in rodent control – a skill they took with them to the pioneering frontiers of the New World causing them to often be seen as a valuable and much prized possession.

The Rise Of The Cat Show

Although cats and mankind had enjoyed some sort of coexisting relationship for many thousands of years, it was not until the mid-nineteenth century that the concept of the selectively bred pedigree cat began to take hold – a stark contrast to the timeline of the domestic dog whose varied sizes, skills and abilities had seen it bred for specific tasks for many centuries. The cat, whilst often an accomplished mouser, was still just a cat and, whilst some owners armed with knowledge of their own feline companions' exploits might beg to differ, did not naturally possess the attributes required for hunting large quarry, guarding livestock or retrieving wildfowl. No, the cat's rise to greatness was triggered by an altogether different desire – the creation of an object that displayed both beauty and elegance.

One person to recognise this burgeoning rise in the feline popularity was the artist and author Harrison Weir. Thinking of the large number of cats kept in London alone, Weir said that he conceived "that it would be well to hold Cat Shows, so that the different breeds, colours, markings etc., might be more carefully attended to". Through

his organisation, the first *official* cat show took place at London's Crystal Palace on 16 July 1871 where he, his brother John Jenner Weir and the Reverend J C Macdona (better known as a canine aficionado and supporter of the St Bernard dog) presided as judges. The show, packed full of interested spectators and declared a resounding success, attracted 170 entrants spread over 25 classes from which prizes were awarded to 32 gentlemen, 15 married ladies and four spinsters! Although the majority of the classes were judged to a strict breed standard diligently created by Weir himself, there were also novelty prizes including one for the biggest cat and one for the fattest!

With cat shows increasing in popularity and becoming regular events the National Cat Club was formed in 1887 with none other than Harrison Weir as its president. Weir, however, soon handed over the reins of power to fellow artist Louis Wain after he began to feel that its members were more interested in winning prizes than promoting feline welfare. The NCC remained the principal authority for pedigree cat breeds and shows until

1910 when it was superseded by the newly formed Governing Council of the Cat Fancy – the organisation which oversees feline affairs in the United Kingdom until this day.

In the United States, much like in Britain, unofficial cat shows had been held at local county fairs for many years before the country's first National Cat Show was held at New York's Madison Square Garden in 1895. Organised by an Englishman, James T Hyde, it attracted an entry of 176 cats exhibited by 125 owners. Several attempts followed which attempted to form a national association; the first of these – the American Cat Club – was formed in 1896 and sought to maintain and publish a stud book and registry of domestic animals in the United States and Canada. America, however, is a large nation and others similarly attempted to achieve the same goal with the Beresford Cat Club (named after the noted English breeder and benefactor Lady Marcus Beresford) and the Chicago Cat Club leading the way. Finally, in 1906, the American Cat Association was formed, becoming the Cat Fanciers' Association (CFA) two years later in 1908.

Since that time many other registries have been formed worldwide. In addition to the GCCF and CFA the principal bodies are the *Fédération Internationale Féline (FIFé)* – the world's largest feline organisation to which many national registries are affiliated – and the International Cat Association (TICA).

Times Change

Despite the wide variety of sizes, shapes, colours and coats the world's domestic cat population can essentially be broken down into two clear groups – those breeds which have emerged naturally over the years and those which have been artificially developed by man by the means of selective breeding.

Many of the naturally occurring breeds still in existence are those which, for many years, enjoyed an isolated existence such as the tailless Manx and the Japanese Bobtail. Others, including the Shorthairs, Maine Coon and the Siberian, developed naturally through free breeding into types that were only formally recognised with the advent of the cat clubs and fancies.

In recent years many new stunning breeds have been engineered through highly controlled selective breeding programmes to a point where there are now far more "artificial" breeds in existence than there are natural ones. The world of selective breeding has not been without its critics – often when breeds are created from a relatively small gene pool they can become highly

susceptible to health problems. However, with time there has come a greater scientific understanding of the issues involved and, in general, the world's cat population now enjoys a healthier existence than ever before.

Notes On Coats

With such a wide variety of colours, patterns and textures the world of the feline coat can be a confusing one for even the most experienced and knowledgeable cat fanatic.

There are three types of hair in a cat's coat: guard hairs, otherwise known as the topcoat, are the coarsest and most protective offering a water-repellent covering that adds the characteristic sheen to a feline coat; awn hairs which are bristly in nature and provide an insulating layer and, finally, soft and curly down hairs which nestle closest to the animal's skin. Different breeds have different coat types made up of varying combinations of length and density of the three different hair types. A British Shorthair, for example, will have approximately 50mm long guard hairs but few, if any, awn hairs. A curly coated Cornish Rex will, by contrast be almost devoid of guard hairs but will display an excess of curly awn and down hairs of similar length.

There are countless varieties of coat pattern, the most common of which are Tabby, Self, Tortoiseshell, Bicolour,

Tricolour and Colourpoint.

Tabby is the most common coat pattern and harks back to the days before domestication when cats lived wild and relied on this cunning camouflage scheme to conceal them whilst on the hunt. There are four varieties of Tabby marking – Mackerel (a striped pattern), Marbled (an uneven blotchy pattern), spotted and agouti.

Self coloureds are by far the most easy to recognise as the coat is of a single colour that is distributed evenly across the whole body. It is not uncommon for kittens to display the odd hairs of another colour before becoming self coloured as they mature.

Tortoiseshell, or Tortie, coats display an evenly distributed mixture of red, cream and black hairs to form a brindled pattern. This pattern is created by a genetic anomaly and is normally only found in females.

Bicolour coats are those that are made up of white plus one other colour which may be either a solid (self) or tabby pattern. This coat pattern is common in mixed-breed cats but is also found in a number of pedigree breeds. A variation of the bicolour is the Van – a cat which is

mostly white apart from small patches of colour on its head and tail.

The Tricolour pattern is made up of a combination of white, black and red or, occasionally, their diluted variations of blue and cream. In the United Kingdom these are commonly known as Tortoiseshell and White whilst in the United States the term Calico is frequently used.

Colourpoint markings are also easy to spot. In this distinctive pattern the face, tail and paws, known as the tips and points, are darker in colour than the coat on the rest of the body. These points can be in various colours many of which carry their own specific names; dark brown markings, for example, are known as seal points whilst red markings are known as flame points.

Abyssinian

Abyssinian	
Place of Origin	Egypt / Ethiopia
Date of Origin	1860s
Other Names	Aby, Bunny Cat
Weight	4 – 7.5kg
Lifespan	9 – 15 years
Temperament	Intelligent and loyal

Whether it is a true incarnation of the goddess Bast or just a humble housecat with unusual origins, the Abyssinian remains one of the most popular breeds of today. Over 3,000 years old and one of the earliest of all breeds known to man, it is said to have originated in Abyssinia (now called Ethiopia). The domestic breed as we know it is said to have been descended from a cat called Zula who was brought to British shores by the wife of army officer Captain Barrett-Leonard at the end of the Abyssinian Campaign in 1868 and then cross bred with an ordinary tabby. The Abyssinian was recognised as a breed in Britain in 1882 before first being exhibited at Crystal Palace a year later.

A medium sized breed, the Abyssinian is intelligent, naturally curious and thrives

Fun Facts

With its regal looks it is little wonder that the Ancient Egyptians are said to have worshipped this creature, in fact more than 300,000 mummified cats were found when the temple at Per–Bast was excavated in the late nineteenth century.

on human company, forming a close and extremely loyal bond with its family. They tolerate other cats well but are known to create a particularly strong attachment to family dogs. They like to be highly active and hate being confined for long periods of time. Abyssinians are adept climbers and enjoy environments in which there are plenty of opportunities for them to look upon others from on high.

American Shorthair

American Shorthair	
Place of Origin	United States
Date of Origin	1900
Other Names	Domestic Shorthair
Weight	3.5 – 7kg
Lifespan	15 – 20 years
Temperament	Gentle and independent

Fun Facts

The first official member of the Domestic Shorthair breed was an orange tabby called Champion Belle of Bradford – an import from England!

Just like the early trappers of the north, the cattlemen of the plains and the transcontinental railroad workers, the American Shorthair cat is one of the true building blocks of American history. There is evidence to suggest that the Pilgrim Fathers utilised cats aboard the Mayflower to control rodents on its journey to the New World and that on arriving in what was to become Massachusetts their mouse-catching skills were put to good use on the newly created farms.

Over the generations, these cats gradually adapted to the sometimes harsh conditions of the North American climate – becoming larger in size, more self-confident and developing thicker coats. With a whole continent to tame, these cats soon became a valuable commodity to a point where, during the California Gold Rush of 1849, mousers were changing hands for upwards of $50 – that's almost $1200 in today's currency!

By the start of the twentieth century, examples of the working cats started to appear at cat shows, however, classed as "Domestic Shorthairs", they struggled to compete against the seemingly more glamorous foreign imports. Only following the Second World War did the breed start to win awards at American cat shows. Considering the use of the word "domestic" to be a potential hindrance to the breed's success, it was renamed the American Shorthair in 1965.

American Shorthairs are gentle and affectionate in nature. Their strong muscular build, hardy nature and general amiability make them particularly good with children and a first class choice as a family pet. They are fairly active but are not of a type likely to spend all day following you around the house. Importantly, they are an outdoorsy breed who cherish their freedom.

American Wirehair

The frizzy-coated American Wirehair is a truly distinctive breed and still quite rare breed that was first discovered on Council Rock Farm in Verona, New York during March of 1966. Nathan Mosher, a bull breeder of some repute, was the owner of two quite standard non-pedigree domestic shorthairs named Bootsie and Fluffy who became the proud parents of a litter of six kittens. One of these, later named Adam, was a curious red-and-white male with a meagre wiry coat and whose hair was coiled and springy right down to the whiskers on his nose.

Word of the arrival of this unusual kitten reached Joan O'Shea, a local breeder of Siamese, Havana Browns

and Rex who, after some lengthy negotiations, convinced Mosher to part with the 10-week-old kitten. A subsequent chance mating between Adam and a brown tabby and white female led to the arrival of two further red-and-white curly-coated kittens. Breeders Madeline and Bill Beck joined O'Shea in promoting this new and unusual breed and were instrumental in getting the American Wirehair recognised by the Cat Fanciers' Association in 1967.

American Wirehairs are sweet by nature and often display a warm and loving personality but are not prone to being clingy. They are energetic and playful without becoming hyperactive and love to be involved in every aspect of your day to day activities. Although they can make an exceptional household pet it should be noted that Wirehairs tend not to enjoy being picked up and cuddled.

American Wirehair

Place of Origin	United States
Date of Origin	1966
Other Names	None
Weight	3.5 – 7kg
Lifespan	15 years
Temperament	Playful and affectionate

Asian

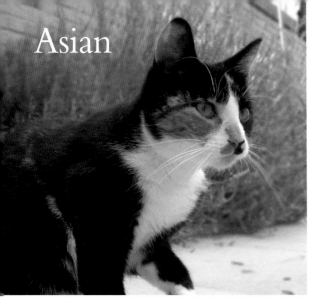

matings producing a wide range of coat lengths, colours and patterns.

With a silver under-coat running between one-third and one-half of the length of its solid coloured top-coat, the Asian Smoke is the most incredible looking cat. Although often mistaken for a self (solid) coloured cat, its appearance comes into its own once it is in motion. Asian Tabbies can have any of four different coat patterns – Classic, Mackerel, Spotted or Ticked. The lovely Asian Self can also be found in a wide range of colours from the stunning Blues and Lilacs through to the soft Creams and Caramels and, of course, the unusual Tortoiseshells (a pattern almost

Rather than being a single breed, the Asian is a group of feline varieties including the Burmilla, the Bombay, the longhaired Tiffanie plus the Asian Smoke, the Asian Tabby and the Asian Self and Tortoiseshell. The breeds all developed from an unintentional mating between a Lilac Burmese and a Chinchilla in 1981. The resulting litter, the property of breeder Miranda Bickford-Smith (née Baroness von Kirchberg) instantly became the basis of the popular Burmilla breed *(see page 62)* with subsequent

Fun Facts

The original clandestine Burmese-Chinchilla meeting between Bambino Lilac Fabergé and Jemari Sanquist took place when both were waiting to be bred in the same building and a cleaner inadvertently left open a connecting door. Animal passion took over and the rest, as they say, is history!

exclusively found only in females).

Asian cats are extremely friendly and show a great deal of warmth. They love being shown affection and relish taking part in all family activities. Whilst these cats can become quite demanding and vocal if ignored they respond well to being spoken to. This is a breed that loves to play and to explore and care should always be taken to ensure that their wandering tendencies do not take them too far from home.

For Bombay Cats see page 50.

Asian	
Place of Origin	United Kingdom
Date of Origin	1981
Other Names	None
Weight	4 – 7kg
Lifespan	> 15 years
Temperament	Affectionate but demanding

Balinese

If you think that the Balinese looks rather like a longhaired Siamese then you would be pretty much right. Although the occasional longhaired Siamese kitten had appeared in litters since the early twentieth century – the result of a parent carrying a recessive mutant longhair gene – it was not until just after the Second World War that intentional breeding and promotion of the type commenced. Almost simultaneously, Californian breeder Marion Dorsey and New Yorker Helen Smith found longhairs amongst their Siamese litters. Rather than pass these on as pets as had been the tradition, both decided to begin

Fun Facts

The name Balinese was originally coined by breeder Helen Smith who thought that "Long Hair Siamese" did not do the graceful appearance of this cat the poetic justice it deserved. She chose the name as she thought they resembled the elegance of a Balinese dancer.

line breeding to perfect this attractive feline. The breed was recognised in the United States in 1961 but did not achieve championship status in the United Kingdom until 1986.Balinese are intelligent and easy going cats that enjoy all company whether human or animal – they are, in fact, particularly fond of dogs and will often sleep curled up with their favourite and let themselves be groomed and nuzzled. They enjoy being extrovert and like nothing better than a good session of highly active play – for this reason they cope easily with the noise and fervour of a room full of children. Their long, soft hair and relaxed and affectionate nature make them ideal for keeping a lap warm during the winter months.

There is one thing, however, that must always be remembered about Balinese – they are the Houdini of the cat world seemingly capable of picking locks, opening doors and generally contorting themselves into the most impossible of shapes in order to get to wherever they think the most interesting things are happening.

Balinese	
Place of Origin	United States
Date of Origin	1940s
Other Names	Javanese (USA)
Weight	2.5 – 5kg
Lifespan	12 years
Temperament	Intelligent, affectionate and extrovert

Bengal

ew other cats can display quite the same level of untamed good looks as the stunning Bengal. A relatively new breed, it was first developed in the United States during the mid- Seventies by Californian Jean Mills who experimented with crossing an Asian Leopard Cat with a domestic cat – originally Abyssinians, Egyptian Maus and Ocicats. Her objective was to develop a practical and pleasant

domestic breed that still retained a strong physical resemblance to its long legged and long bodied wild ancestor.

One thing that truly makes the Bengal stand out from the crowd is its distinctive coat which displays both an unusual marbled pattern of random swirls found in no other domestic breed and an equally unique pearl or gold dusting that gives it an amazing glittery sheen. This glorious coat feels as good as

it looks – its soft, dense, silkiness making it possible to identify, according to many owners, even when blindfolded.

Although nocturnal by nature, Bengals can adjust well to the hubbub of domestic life. Athletic to the extreme and highly intelligent they are impressive natural hunters and, unusually for a feline breed, display a particular affinity to dogs and to water, loving to play with both at any given opportunity. It should always be remembered that the Bengal is a specialist cat with specialist needs and is, therefore, not ideally suited to the novice owner. However, given the appropriate time, care and attention they can make an outstanding contribution to any household.

Bengal

Place of Origin	United States
Date of Origin	1983
Other Names	Leopardettes
Weight	5.5 – 10kg
Lifespan	9 – 15 years
Temperament	Self assured and energetic

Birman

Birman	
Place of Origin	Myanmar (Burma)
Date of Origin	Unknown – Possibly ancient
Other Names	Sacred Birman
Weight	4.5 – 8kg
Lifespan	> 15 years
Temperament	Gentle and easy to handle

The ancient history of the magnificent Birman is surrounded in legend and mystery. It is said that many years ago on the side of Mount Lugh in Burma (now known as Myanmar) there was a temple dedicated to Tsun Kyan-Kse, a sapphire-eyed goddess who presided over passage of souls. One-hundred cats, all white with amber eyes, lived within the temple to act as both guards and companions. One night the temple was attacked by raiders from Siam who slew Mun-Ha, the elderly head priest of the community. As he lay dying Sinh, his favourite cat, jumped onto his head and sat before the statue of the goddess. Incredibly the cat began to change in appearance taking on a golden coat whilst its nose, ears and legs turned brown like the earth. Its paws, which had touched the dying priest, remained the purest white whilst its eyes became sapphire blue like those of Tsun Kyan-Kse. A week later the remaining 99 cats also underwent the same transformation.

Whilst the legend might stretch the imagination a little the story of how the Birman came to reside in the west is more straightforward. It is known that a pair of Birmans was sent from Burma to France in

1919 as a gift to an English army officer called Major Gordon Russell. One of the cats died en route but the other, which was already in kitten, survived and gave birth to its litter in France.

The Birman is affectionate and gentle by nature and loves being around people to a point where it will follow you from room to room to enjoy your company. They take well to being handled and mix with other cats without too many problems. Particularly fond of children, they can make a good, if slightly unusual, family pet.

Bombay

Bombay	
Place of Origin	United States
Date of Origin	1960s
Other Names	Mini Panther
Weight	2.5 – 5kg
Lifespan	> 15 years
Temperament	Social, intelligent and playful

The Bombay was first created by American breeder Nikki Horner of the Shawnee Cattery in Louisville, Kentucky. Dreaming of creating an all black Asian type but with copper eyes, she first bred a black American Shorthair to a sable Burmese in 1958 but her results were unsuccessful. In 1962 she tried once more – this time with great success. There followed a period of selective breeding from which Mrs Horner was consistently able to produce elegant

cats with shimmering satin-like ebony coats, huge copper eyes and a very distinctive head and body – its miniature resemblance to the Indian black leopard earning it the name of Bombay. In 1976, 18 years after Nikki Horner's first breeding experiments, the Bombay gained official recognition in the United States although they did not achieve full championship status in the United Kingdom until 1999.

The Bombay is a highly intelligent breed that hankers for human companionship at every opportunity and hates being left on its own. Chatty and vocal they thoroughly enjoy holding extended conversations with their owners whom they invariably shadow everywhere they go. They like to play games and are natural born retrievers who love to show off and perform tricks.

Fun Facts

In France the Bombay is known as a Matagot or Magician Cat and is said to bring good luck to its owners.

British Shorthair

Although active development of the British Shorthair only commenced in earnest during the second half of the nineteenth century the breed has existed in one form or another for many hundreds of years. The Romans brought shorthair cats to British shores in the first century AD and they have since featured in countless paintings, engravings and illustrations. Once the classic farm and street cat, the best examples were interbred before first being shown at the Crystal Palace show in 1871. With ever more exotic cats becoming the vogue in the early part of the twentieth century the British Shorthair gradually fell from favour, however, following the Second World War it staged a recovery with breeders crossing the type with Persian cats improving coat thickness and enhancing its thickset look.

The British Shorthair is a big softie at heart. Loving and affectionate, they are more than happy curling up tight on a conveniently placed lap but do not demand the constant company and attention that is seen with many of their more exotic cousins. They are good with children and, if properly introduced, can socialise well with other animals. This is a big cat that needs to eat well but it should, however, be recognised that they are prone to obesity so careful dietary control is still required.

British Shorthair	
Place of Origin	United Kingdom
Date of Origin	1880s
Other Names	Various – Colour specific
Weight	4 – 8kg
Lifespan	12 – 13 years
Temperament	Affectionate but not needy

British Black Shorthair

Of the British Shorthair breed, one of the most popular variations is the British Black Shorthair – at one time, however, this was far from the case. Historically, in many societies, the shorthaired black cat was treated with a great deal of suspicion and as an object of fear. During the Middle Ages it was often thought that witches used them as familiars and could change into them by casting a spell or that the devil himself would walk amongst mortals disguised as a black cat. This led, on holy days, to many of the poor creatures being hunted down and burned. Fortunately in the United Kingdom this trend was turned

British Black Shorthair	
Place of Origin	United Kingdom
Date of Origin	1880s
Other Names	None
Weight	4 – 8kg
Lifespan	12 – 13 years
Temperament	Affectionate and intelligent

Fun Facts

For many years, black cats have been the root of numerous nautical superstitions. In Yorkshire, fishermen's wives would keep a black cat in the house to guarantee the safe return of their husbands and sailors would keep them as they were supposed to ensure fair weather and a safe journey.

around and the sighting of a black cat, especially one crossing your path, was seen as a good omen of things to come.

Originally produced by selectively breeding from the very best street cats, the British Black Shorthair was one of the very first breeds to be shown at the Crystal Palace show during the latter half of the nineteenth century. Shorthaired black cats are, of course, a relatively common sight, however, most of these will be of a green eyed variety. It is usually only the pedigree type which possesses the gleaming copper eyes that make this breed appear so stunning.

British Tabby Shorthair

British Tabby Shorthair	
Place of Origin	United Kingdom
Date of Origin	1880s
Other Names	None
Weight	4 – 8kg
Lifespan	12 – 13 years
Temperament	Gentle and affectionate

Harking back to the camouflaged markings of their ancient wild forebears, the Tabby's familiar look means it is often seen as the quintessential domestic cat. However, the stringent breed standard of the British Tabby Shorthair has ensured that, in the show-ring at least, it is far from being a common old moggy.

The Tabby has existed in one form or another for many thousands of years – cats with similar markings can be seen on numerous artworks throughout history with the earliest dating from Ancient Egypt. The name itself also claims Middle Eastern origins having been derived from Al AtTabiya, a quarter of Old Baghdad famed for its rich waved silk cloth known in Britain as tabis or tabbi.

The British Tabby Shorthair is bred in two distinct coat patterns and

Fun Facts

Since 1988 the Tabby has been the official cat of Massachusetts having been nominated by the American state's schoolchildren.

in several colours: brown, red and silver being accepted colours in both the United Kingdom and the United States with blue and cream also being permitted stateside. The Classic Tabby Shorthair should have three stripes running along the length of its spine, a butterfly shape on each shoulder and a large oyster-shaped spiral on each flank. The Mackerel Tabby Shorthair has a striped coat lacking the spirals of the Classic. Both usually have a pronounced M-shaped marking on their forehead.

British Tortoiseshell Shorthair

British Tortoiseshell Shorthair	
Place of Origin	United Kingdom
Date of Origin	1880s
Other Names	Tortie, Spanish Cat or Calico★ ★*with white markings*
Weight	4 – 8kg
Lifespan	12 – 13 years
Temperament	Affectionate and intelligent

Although the Tortoiseshell is relatively common and was one of the very first British Shorthair types to be recognised for showing, it remains one of the most difficult domestic cats to breed. To produce a Tortie, as they are affectionately known, a queen is best mated to a solid-coloured black, cream or red Shorthair male but even this combination does not guarantee the desired offspring – perhaps just a single kitten from the resultant litter will display the correct markings. Due to the nature of the complex genetics that determine this coat colouring, almost all Tortoiseshells are female – those that are male (about 1 in 3,000) are usually found to be sterile.

Other variations of the British Tortoiseshell Shorthair include the Tortoiseshell-and-White – an old breed

Fun Facts

Tortoiseshell Cats will tend to have an even marking all over their coats whilst Tortoiseshell-and-Whites will have big patches of colour.

known formerly as a Spanish Cat or as a Calico in the United States – and the British Blue Tortoiseshell-White – a more recent creation upon which the black and red of the standard type is replaced with blue and cream.

As with the other British Shorthair breeds the Tortoiseshell is an intelligent, affectionate and independent creature capable of being an exceptional house pet.

Burmese

Burmese	
Place of Origin	Myanmar (Burma)
Date of Origin	1930s
Other Names	None
Weight	3.5 – 6.5kg
Lifespan	> 15 years
Temperament	Intelligent and vocal

Unlike its Balinese cousin, the Burmese can truly stake a claim to origins that connect directly with its name. A cat answering the Burmese description can be found in The Cat-Book Poems – an ancient Thai book of paintings and verse created during the Ayudhya Period in Siam (1350-1767) – at which time they were revered and served as dwellers in Buddhist temples.

It is known that Burmese types were shown in the United Kingdom as early as 1871, however, these were, at the time, considered to be Chocolate Siamese and not a true breed in their own right. The breed, as we recognise it, was founded as recently as 1930 after Dr Joseph Cressman

Fun Facts

A Burmese called Tarawood Antigone holds the record for the most kittens born to a single litter. On 7 August 1970, the four-year-old owned by Valerie Gane of Oxfordshire, gave birth to 19 kittens; four of which were stillborn. Of the remaining 15, just a single kitten was female!

Thompson imported a brown female cat called Wong Mau into the United States from Burma. Unable to find a similar male with which to breed, it was crossed with a Seal Point Siamese named Tai Mau. Wong Mau was then bred with her son to produce a litter of dark brown kittens. The breed was recognised in the United States in 1936.

The first of the breed to arrive in the United Kingdom came with British servicemen returning from Burma in 1945 before being recognised by the GCCF in 1952. Although the breed was since bolstered by cross-breeding with American imports, the look of the European Burmese (as it is now known) and the American Burmese is quite different – the European variety being far more muscled and angular in comparison to its trans-Atlantic cousin.

The Burmese is an affectionate and friendly creature that enjoys human company and a domestic environment. They are loyal, highly talkative and enjoy a good cuddle. Their very high intelligence can often lead to them being able to figure out how to open doors and windows so beware as they are quite the escape artists!

Burmilla

Burmilla	
Place of Origin	United Kingdom
Date of Origin	1981
Other Names	Asian Shaded
Weight	4 – 7kg
Lifespan	> 15 years
Temperament	Moderate but attention seeking

It is often said that accidents will happen; this, however doesn't always have to be a bad thing. In 1981 two cats owned by the late

Miranda Bickford-Smith, a Chinchilla stud named Jemari Sanquist and a Lilac Burmese queen called Bambino Lilac Fabergé, indulged in clandestine activities that resulted in a litter of four quite stunning kittens possessing the body of their Burmese mother but with the soft, tipped silver coat of their Chinchilla father. With all four kittens quickly homed, the potential of establishing an all-new breed was soon recognised and, in 1984, the Burmilla Cat Club was formed. The breed became formally recognised by the GCCF in 1995.

The Burmilla's temperament is a happy compromise between those of its genetic forebears – it is less boisterous than a Burmese but more active and inquisitive than a Chinchilla. They are fairly vocal and will spend a good deal of their time following their owners from room to room seeking the attention they consider is rightfully theirs. They enjoy the company of children and will enjoy getting stuck into the rough and tumble of a good play session taking it upon themselves to retreat to quieter confines either when fed up or if the mood happens to take them.

Chartreux

Chartreux	
Place of Origin	France
Date of Origin	Middle Ages
Other Names	None
Weight	3 – 7.5kg
Lifespan	> 15 years
Temperament	Gentle and adaptable

The elegant Chartreux is said to have been developed during the Middle Ages by the Carthusian monks resident at La Grand Chartreuse in the French Alps from feral stock brought back from North Africa by returning Crusaders. Their first documentation dates from the eighteenth century when the French naturalist Georges-Louis Leclerc, Comte de Buffon, detailed the Chat des Chartreux in his extensive work Oeuvres Complètes de Buffon. The breed was first shown during the early twentieth century by the Legers sisters who used animals from the remote Belle-Ile-sur-Mer as the foundation for their line. The Chartreux, however, suffered a decline in popularity leading

Fun Facts

In 1933, the French author Colette described her own Chartreux "Saha" in the book La Chatte. She referred to it as her "little bear with fat cheeks and golden eyes" and her "blue pigeon, her pearl grey devil".

to it becoming almost extinct at the turn of the Second World War when only a concerted effort from some dedicated enthusiasts ensured its long-term survival.

The playful Chartreux can take as long as two years to fully mature with the male becoming much larger and heavier in build compared to the female. Despite its size, it is an extremely agile breed that thoroughly enjoys playing games and hunting. They are a gentle and adaptable type that thoroughly relish human companionship, especially that of children.

In Europe, hybridisation is permitted with the Chartreux being shown in the same category as the familiar British Shorthair. However, in the United States the CFA recognises it as a breed in its own right and has awarded it full championship status.

Cornish Rex

Cornish Rex	
Place of Origin	United Kingdom
Date of Origin	1950s
Other Names	None
Weight	2.5 – 4.5kg
Lifespan	10 – 14 years
Temperament	Demanding and playful

With its thoroughly unusual crinkled coat, the Cornish Rex certainly has no problem in standing out from other breeds. Although similar looking cats had appeared in litters for many years, it was only in 1950 that the breed as we know it started to be defined when Serena, a tortoiseshell and white Shorthair belonging to Mrs Nina Ennismore and Miss Winifred Macalister, gave birth to a litter of five kittens on a farm in Bodmin, Cornwall. Four of the kittens sported normal short coats but a fifth, named Kallibunker, had been born with a tight curly cream coat and whiskers that looked liked coiled watch springs.

Fun Facts

The name Rex is thought to originate from King Albert I of Belgium after he entered some curly-coated rabbits into a show. They failed to meet breed standard but, rather than offend the monarch, they were accepted and had Rex, the Latin for King, written alongside their names.

Under the advice of a local breeder, Kallibunker's owners embarked on a breeding programme which saw the cat bred back to his mother – the result of which produced two more curly coated offspring.

The Cornish Rex is a highly intelligent cat that loves company from humans, other cats and even dogs if introduced at a young age. It demands attention but will be happy left with feline company if its owner is not at home. Gentle by nature they make excellent companions for children if treated with the respect they deserve. They are, however, far from being lap cats and easily prefer a good game of hunt the ping-pong ball than an evening in front of the television. Interestingly, their unusual coat often makes them suitable for owners who would normally suffer from cat allergies although this is not always the case.

Cymric

The Cymric (pronounced kum-rik) is essentially a long-haired variety of the famous tail-less Manx Cat. Its true origin remains unclear – one school of thought suggests that, before being concentrated upon as a potential show breed, it had existed for many years on the Isle of Man alongside its shorthair Manx cousin. Others, however, maintain that it is an offshoot from a programme started in the 1930s whereby Persians were introduced into the Manx breeding line in an attempt to improve coat thickness. Whatever the truth may be, one thing is pretty certain – despite its name, the breed has no connection with Wales! The name was the invention of two pioneering breeders Leslie Falteisek and Blair Wright.

An excellent choice as a pet, the

Fun Facts

Geneticists would tell you otherwise but legend has it that the tail-less Manx and Cymric were the last animals to board the Ark but in his haste to beat the weather Noah slammed the gate shut on their tails.

Cymric is playful, energetic and adores human company with a tendency to gravitate around one particular member of the household. It is often said that they possess many characteristics which are more readily associated with canines rather than cats including an ability to retrieve and a penchant for burying their toys! The Cymric's pièce de résistance is, however, its stunning jumping ability. No fence, no shelf and no curtain rail are out of reach for this seemingly bionic feline.

Cymric	
Place of Origin	North America
Date of Origin	1960s
Other Names	Longhaired Manx
Weight	3.5 – 5.5kg
Lifespan	10 – 14 years
Temperament	Energetic and playful

Devon Rex

For some time, Beryl Cox had admired a large black curly-haired tom who lived wild in a disused tin mine near her home in Buckfastleigh, Devon but it always refused to be tamed preferring, instead, a feral life amongst the local ruins. One day in 1959, however, she noticed that he had mated with another local stray, a tortoiseshell and white female. After a brief search Miss Cox found the litter in a field at the end of her garden and found that one of the kittens, a black

Fun Facts

Rather than sporting whiskers, the Devon Rex wears a feline designer stubble. Its whiskers are so brittle that they rarely grow more than an inch in length.

smoke, also had a curly coat. Naming it Kirlee, she took it home and cared for it.

Respected breeder and show judge Brian Stirling-Webb purchased Kirlee as an addition to his Cornish Rex breeding stock; however, although physically similar to its Cornish cousin, the Devon was established to be a wholly different breed after mating between two types yielded only normal-looking, straight-haired kittens. Stirling-Webb continued to persevere and out-crossed Kirlee to other breeds to expand the Devon gene pool. His efforts gradually bore fruit and within just 10 years the breed had been recognised by the GCCF.

Huge saucer eyes and oversized ears give the adorable Devon Rex a pixie-like expression that separates it from its Cornish neighbour. Often described as "little terrors" they are true acrobats who enjoy climbing wallpaper and swinging from curtains. Loving and biddable, they can be trained to walk out using a harness. Whilst they crave and adore human attention they are not, by any means, lap cats preferring instead to partake in some physical gamesmanship especially if you are good enough to dangle a toy in front of them.

Cornish Rex	
Place of Origin	United Kingdom
Date of Origin	1960s
Other Names	Poodle Cat
Weight	2.5 – 4kg
Lifespan	> 15 years
Temperament	Highly active

Egyptian Mau

Egyptian Mau	
Place of Origin	Egypt / Italy
Date of Origin	Ancient
Other Names	None
Weight	2.25 – 5kg
Lifespan	> 15 years
Temperament	Highly active

It is believed that the elegant Egyptian Mau ancestors were a spotted subspecies of the African Wild Cat that was first domesticated thousands of years ago by the ancient Egyptians who not only cosseted it as a pet and a worker but also worshipped it as a god. A highly similar spotted cat is pictured on a tomb in Thebes dating back to 1400 BC whilst a papyrus from 1100 BC shows the mighty sun-god Ra depicted as a spotted cat beheading an evil serpent.

In its modern form, it is thought to have originated from the environs of the city of Cairo – mau is, quite simply, the Egyptian word for cat – before being introduced to Europe in the early twentieth century where it was developed by avid French, Swiss and Italian breeders. As with many specialist

breeds it all but died out following the ravages of the Second World War but was saved from extinction by Nathalie Troubetskoy, an exiled Russian princess living in Rome who was given a silver spotted kitten in a shoebox by a young acquaintance. Enamoured by this small, seemingly vulnerable creature she researched its history, discovered its significance and then embarked on a quest to rescue the breed.

Even after all of these years, the Mau's hunting and retrieving past rings true with most thinking that there is little better than a good game of fetch. Maus love family life and show extreme loyalty and affection to their keepers but can show disinterest to people they do not know. They are very conversational but tend not to have a loud voice preferring instead to make chortling sounds whilst padding their feet.

Exotic Shorthair

Exotic Shorthair	
Place of Origin	United States
Date of Origin	1960s
Other Names	Shorthaired Persian
Weight	3 – 6.5kg
Lifespan	13 – 15 years
Temperament	Laid back

For many years, fans of American Shorthairs were more than happy with the breed's sturdy good looks and traditional coat colours. But then, in the 1950s, a number of breeders decided to cross their cats with Persians in an attempt to create a better body shape and to introduce the silver colour to their fur. The hybridised cats became extremely popular at shows to a point where many traditional American Shorthair breeders became aggrieved that this new type was proving to be a dominant force. Rather than banning the hybrid type from competition, the suggestion was made that they should be allowed to compete in a category of their own and in 1967 the breed was awarded championship status in the United States under the name of Exotic Shorthair.

Fun Facts

Before settling on Exotic Shorthair as a name for the breed it was suggested that "Sterling" would be an appropriate choice because of the silvery colouring that had been introduced.

Although highly affectionate and loyal, Exotics generally display a laid back attitude to life. Given the chance, they are always keen to play a game or two and will indulge in a session of string chasing with great enthusiasm. However, once this is all done and dusted they like nothing more than to stretch out and enjoy a good, long sleep – preferably at the end of your very own bed!

Havana

Havana	
Place of Origin	United Kingdom
Date of Origin	1950s
Other Names	Havana Brown
Weight	2.5 – 4.5kg
Lifespan	> 15 years
Temperament	Charming and inquisitive

Of British origin, the Havana is essentially a manmade breed although it is known that self-brown Siamese type cats existed across Europe during the late nineteenth century and that the eleventh edition of the Encyclopaedia Britannica, published in 1911, makes mention of a "wholly chocolate-coloured strain of Siamese" – the type often being known as the Swiss Mountain Cat. This early strain of the breed, however, met an unfortunate and early demise when, in 1920, the officious Siamese Cat Club of Britain issued a declaration that it was "unable to encourage the breeding of any but

Fun Facts

The GCCF originally decided to name the breed the Chestnut Brown Foreign. It was not until 1970 that the Council agreed to the name being changed to Havana Brown. In the United Kingdom the "Brown" part was later dropped, however, the breed continues to be known as the Havana Brown in the United States.

blue-eyed Siamese". Excluded from all Siamese showing classes, the breed soon fell by the wayside.

Fortunately, in 1951, a small but dedicated group of British breeders set about reviving the solid, or self, coloured brown cat and it is from here that the modern breed originates. The first brown male, Elmtower Bronze Idol, was born in 1952 with two more in 1953 to form the foundation of the breed in the United Kingdom. The breed gained GCCF recognition in 1958 with the CFA following suit in the United States just a year later.

The Havana, said to be named after the colour of a fine Havana cigar, is a charming and playful creature with a highly curious nature. It is said that a sound that would make most felines flee in terror is nothing but an invitation to this breed! Soft of voice and highly affectionate, they are perfect for anybody looking for an intelligent and independent companion – especially if they are a chocolate lover!

Japanese Bobtail

Japanese Bobtail	
Place of Origin	Japan
Date of Origin	8th Century
Other Names	None
Weight	2.5 – 4kg
Lifespan	13 – 15 years
Temperament	Friendly and vocal

The Japanese Bobtail is a curious breed known best for its highly unusual bobbed tail that resembles that normally found on a rabbit. This veteran breed can be traced as far back as the eighth century and the Heian period of Japanese history and was later recorded in Kaempfer's Japan – a book written by German doctor Englebert Kaempfer in the eighteenth century that is considered to be the first text written by a European about Japan's varied flora and fauna. He observed that "It has no mind to hunt for rats and mice and just wants to be stroked and carried by women".

There are many legends surrounding the reasons why the Bobtail lost its tail. A popular story tells of how a cat was warming itself by a fire when it got too close to the flames and ignited its tail. As it ran through the streets

Fun Facts

Considered a bringer of good luck, many homes, offices and stores in Japan have a statue of a friendly looking Bobtail called a Maneki Neko, or beckoning cat.

aflame it set fire to many buildings. In punishment the Emperor decreed that all cats should have their tails cut off.

Intelligent and extremely friendly, the Bobtail makes an excellent companion or family pet. They are highly vocal and possess a wide range of softly spoken tones that lead some fans to claim that they can sing – extremely polite they will invariably speak when spoken to! They love to carry things in their mouths and relish the opportunity to demonstrate their unsurpassed pouncing power with a lively game of fetch.

Korat

Originating in Siam, the Korat is one of the world's oldest natural breeds. The earliest known depiction of the breed can be found in the famous Cat Book Poems created during the early Ayudhya period of Siamese history in which it tells how "The hairs are smooth, with roots like clouds and tips like silver. The eyes shine like dewdrops on a lotus leaf". During the nineteenth century, King Rama V commissioned a copy of the book on special Khoi paper. On viewing the completed facsimile, King Rama V commented "what a pretty cat – where is this from?" The reply was "Korat Province" – and so the breed was named.

Although details are unclear, it is thought that the first Korat seen outside of Japan was Nam Noi, the property of a Mrs Spearman and imported in January of 1895.

Fun Facts

In their native Thailand Korats are given in pairs to newlywed couples as a symbol of fertility and good luck.

A year later the cat was shown at Holland House in London as a Blue Siamese where it was to be judged by the renowned artist Louis Wain. Unfortunately Mr Wain took umbrage and refused to mark it stating that, as it was not biscuit coloured it could only be considered "an inferior quality Siamese".

Sadly Korats remained unseen in the west until the late 1950s when American breeder Jean Johnson received two cats, Nara and Dara, from a friend in Bangkok. It was not, however, seen again in the United Kingdom until the 1970s.

Gregarious by nature, the Korat tends to be playful and fun loving when it is getting its own way however, this is a breed that can blow hot and cold and if ignored or upset it can demonstrate a near unparalleled stubborn streak and become very territorial. It is intelligent and gentle preferring a quiet household to one full of hustle, bustle and noise.

Korat	
Place of Origin	Siam (Thailand)
Date of Origin	16th Century
Other Names	Si–Sawat
Weight	2.5 – 5kg
Lifespan	18 – 19 years
Temperament	Outgoing but stubborn

Maine Coon

Maine Coon	
Place of Origin	United States
Date of Origin	1860s
Other Names	Main Shag, Coon Cat
Weight	4 – 10kg
Lifespan	13 – 15 years
Temperament	Friendly and playful

America's oldest breed of cat, the Maine Coon, unsurprisingly originates from the state of Maine in the far north east of the country. Its ancestors were most likely longhaired cats brought back by traders and seafarers from foreign lands that mated with strong local shorthair breeds to produce robust, heavily built cats with thick, long coats and bushy, ringed tails not unlike those found on racoons. These arbitrary encounters produced cats of all patterns and colours – their coats becoming progressively thicker over the generations as natural protection from the harsh winter weather notorious in the region.

The breed is one of the earliest to have been shown in the United States, making its debut at the 1860 New York Cat Show before being registered a year later. Although popular as a house cat for many years, it gradually fell from favour over the first half of the twentieth century as Persians were introduced into the United States. The formation of the Central Maine Cat Club in 1953 and a resurgence of interest from a small but dedicated band of breeders have since ensured its

return to grace.

The Maine Coon is a surprisingly

heavyweight cat that can often weigh up to 10 kg. They are friendly and playful and thoroughly enjoy human company. Although not generally talkative they are notable for making a quiet chirping sound when seeking attention or showing contentment. If you happen to own a Maine Coon and are having trouble locating it, the best advice is to look in the most unlikely places – its ancestor's ability to sleep rough has not been lost through the generations!

Manx

It may seem an obvious thing to say, but we have to thank the Isle of Man for the Manx cat. That is not to say that the unusual breed's origins were wholly based on the 221-square-mile island that stands equidistant between England, Ireland and Scotland in the shimmering Irish Sea – only that its geographical exile allowed the Manx's gene pool to develop unfettered.

Many legends surround how the Manx cat lost its tail. Stories tell of how a tailless feline swam ashore from a sinking Spanish man-o-war that had been part of the Armada of 1588 or of the Irish raiders who chopped off cat's tails to wear as plumes in their helmets. The reality is, however, somewhat more down to earth – the taillessness resulting

Manx	
Place of Origin	Isle of Man
Date of Origin	Pre 1700s
Other Names	Rumpy
Weight	3.5 – 5.5kg
Lifespan	10 – 12 years
Temperament	Even tempered and affectionate

Fun Facts

Celebrated artist JMW Turner (1775-1851) was a dedicated fan of the Manx cat owning seven of the curious creatures which wandered unchecked, often with wet feet, over unhung watercolours in his gallery. It is even said that one of his works acted as a makeshift catflap!

from nothing more than a mutant gene.

Similar in many respects to the British Shorthair, a true Manx, usually referred to as a Rumpy, should have no tail whatsoever – instead possessing a small hole where it should have been. Some members of the breed, however, survive with a small remaining tail, called Stumpies, Stubbies or Longies depending on its length.

The Manx is a good natured, even-tempered, affectionate and highly adaptable creature that makes an exceptional pet. They get on extremely well with other animals, especially dogs, and look forward to getting stuck in with all family activities. They show a curious affinity with water and are capable of jumping far higher than you would ever imagine.

Mixed Breeds – Non Pedigree

With all of the attention lavished on the numerous pedigree breeds it can be easy to forget the humble moggie. It is, however, these non-pedigree creatures that make up the vast majority of the world's feline population. All cats share the same illustrious bloodlines that run far back into the depths of time when they were worshipped as deities and revered by kings and queens.

Pedigree shorthaired cats have, for example, only been differentiated from their non-pedigree cousins since the middle of the nineteenth century when, with the advent of the cat fancy, the street cats with the best colouring, marking and confirmation were selectively bred for the burgeoning pastime of showing. Their longhaired cousins were mostly descended from Persian and Turkish cats which, in turn, either crossbred with other longhairs or found liaison with shorthaired cats; however, with the shorthair gene being dominant, longhair non-pedigree cats are a rarity. With all non-pedigree cats, the most commonly seen markings are those of the Tabby. Carried in a dominant gene, this basic feline pattern forms an excellent natural camouflage coating that is ideal for hunting. Almost invariably, the non-pedigree breeds will display a more rugged demeanour and hardy constitution than their show-ring bred counterparts.

When all is said and done, it is often the non-pedigree moggie that can make for the best household pet. Although tough and resilient, they show no less intelligence, affection and loyalty as their aristocratic relations. After all, on a cold winters evening, does it really matter what breed the warm ball of fur curled up on your lap actually is?

Mixed Breed

Place of Origin	Anywhere
Date of Origin	4000BC
Other Names	Moggie
Weight	3.5 – 7kg
Lifespan	12 – 15 years
Temperament	Affectionate

Munchkin

The world's smallest cat is Heed. Born in 2006, this little black and white Munchkin stood just 8 cm tall when 14 weeks old and could happily conceal himself behind a drinks can!

The delightful Munchkin is a naturally occurring domestic breed characterised by its unusually short legs. Although a recent addition as a registered breed, examples of vertically challenged felines have been recorded since the 1940s with sightings in Great Britain, Germany and Russia where it became known as the "Stalingrad Kangaroo Cat" due to its propensity for sitting back on its haunches and waving its paws in the air.

Although this European strain seems to be no more, the type was rediscovered in 1983 in Rayville, Louisiana, when teacher Sandra Hochenedel found two female cats huddled together under a pickup truck cornered by an inquisitive bulldog. She rescued both and, realising that they were pregnant, decided to keep one, which she named Blackberry, and re-home the other, named Blueberry.

It was immediately obvious that both cats had an unusual appearance – sporting short, stubby legs – but further surprises were afoot when their subsequent litters showed the same attribute. Hochenedel and a friend, Kay LaFrance, who had been given a Blackberry kitten as a gift, contacted TICA's genetics committee in 1990. After studying the cats it was revealed that the short legs were the result of

a genetic mutation and was inherited by a dominant gene. The breed was introduced to the public in 1991 and was accepted by TICA in 1994. Named after the tiny inhabitants of Munchkinland from the 1939 classic The Wizard of Oz, the breed has gone from strength to strength but still remains unrecognised by certain federations (including the GCCF).

Despite its diminutive stature, the self-assured Munchkin is capable of running as fast as any normal sized domestic cat – moving with what has often been described as a ferret-like bounce. They can also climb and jump with the best of their contemporaries.

They are sweet in nature, highly confident and show great affection to their human companions.

Munchkin	
Place of Origin	United States
Date of Origin	1983
Other Names	None
Weight	2.5 – 4kg
Lifespan	12 – 15 years
Temperament	Lively and affectionate

Nebelung

When visitors attended the very first British cat shows in the second half of the nineteenth century, many were wowed by the elegant body and stunning luminescent long blue coat of the Russian Longhair. Over time, its shorthair cousin became known as the Russian Blue; the Longhair, however, lost its separate identity with the formation of the modern cat fancies.

Inspired by the striking images of these eye-catching creatures, American breeder Cora Cobb of Denver, Colorado set to recreating the breed by mating her black American Shorthair, Elsa, to an unregistered male that possessed the appearance of a Russian Blue. Of the resulting litter of six black and blue shorthair kittens, one male was a blue longhair. Five months later Elsa produced a litter of seven kittens, one of which was a similar blue longhair but, this time, female. Named Siegfried and Brunhilde after characters from the epic German poem Nibelungenlied, the inspiration for composer Richard Wagner's Ring Cycle (Der Ring des Nibelungen), the two progeny were then mated to produce a litter of

wonderful semi-longhaired blue kittens. With the assistance of Dr Solvfeig Pflueger of TICA's genetics commission, the new breed was developed to the same standard as the Russian before finally becoming recognised in 1987.

The Nebelung is an unassuming, quiet and intelligent cat but is often shy and nervous of strangers. They do, however, show a great deal of affection for their owners often shadowing them from room to room and making instant use of any conveniently placed lap.

Nebelung	
Place of Origin	United States
Date of Origin	1986
Other Names	None
Weight	2.25 – 5kg
Lifespan	12 – 15 years
Temperament	Shy and retiring

Norwegian Forest

Norwegian Forest	
Place of Origin	Norway
Date of Origin	1930s
Other Names	Norse, Skogkatt, Wegie
Weight	3 – 9kg
Lifespan	10 – 12 years
Temperament	Attention seeking

The Norwegian Forest Cat originates, as its name would suggest, from the Nordic fjords. It is a very old breed that is thought to have developed from the mating of shorthair cats carried home from Britain by returning Vikings, longhair types brought back from the Crusades and local feral cats. Over the centuries, it has become a very rugged breed and has adapted well to the harsh, sub-zero temperatures of the Scandinavian winters developing along the way a special double coat which is not only capable of keeping the piercing winds at bay but is also quick drying and provides ample protection from the heavy snows of the region.

For many centuries considered nothing more than a domestic house

cat, the Norwegian Forest was first recognised in its native land in the early 1930s, however, the showing of a small number of Skogkatten in Germany in the latter part of the decade raised considerable interest. Unfortunately, as with so many other breeds, the onset of the Second World War put paid to its emerging status and it lay, almost forgotten, until resurgence in popularity in the early 1970s led to it receiving the international recognition it truly deserved.

Wegies, as they are affectionately known, love attention and utterly thrive on human company. They insist on being acknowledged and can be very demanding of your time. Used to the rigours of outdoor existence, they are more than happy to be left to roam outside but will equally take to the offer of a warm lap in front of an open fire.

Ocicat

Ocicat	
Place of Origin	United States
Date of Origin	1964
Other Names	Oci
Weight	2.5 – 6.5kg
Lifespan	18 – 19 years
Temperament	Devoted and extrovert

For all of the carefully planned selective breeding involved in the world of the cat fancy, sometimes the best creatures are nothing more than the happy result of an accidental mating or a quirk of nature. One such feline is the delightful Ocicat – an elegant but wild-looking spotted feline created more by luck than judgement by American breeder Virginia Daly following the mating of a Seal Point Siamese and an Abyssinian. Her intention was to produce an Aby-pointed Siamese, but what she actually got was a kitten whose gold-spotted ivory coat gave it the appearance of a small wild Ocelot – hence the name Ocicat was coined. Over the following

years, Mrs Daly continued to develop the breed, introducing, as she did, American Shorthair bloodlines into the breeding programme to create a stronger bone and a more muscular stature. The breed achieved championship status in the United States in 1987 before first being introduced to the United Kingdom a year later.

Although Ocicats may look like a wild cat in appearance, they have proved to be more dog-like in nature, becoming highly devoted to their owners, enjoying human company and insisting on playing games. They are intelligent, curious and extrovert and cope particularly well in the company of children if given the respect they are due.

Oriental Shorthair

Oriental Shorthair	
Place of Origin	United Kingdom
Date of Origin	1950s
Other Names	Foreign Type
Weight	4 – 6.5kg
Lifespan	> 15 years
Temperament	Intelligent and inquisitive

In physical shape and temperament, the Oriental Shorthair is exactly the same as a Siamese – the only notable difference being the colouring of its coat and eyes. When, in the latter half of the nineteenth century, the first Siamese type cats were imported into the United Kingdom from Siam (now Thailand) both pointed and self (solid) colours were noted. However, over years of domestic breeding it was the blue–eyed pointed type that gained favour, leading to the Siamese Club of Britain declaring in 1920 that it was "unable to encourage the breeding of all but blue-eyed Siamese".

Numbers of the non-blue eyed Siamese gradually dwindled although it is thought that blues and blacks may have been bred in Germany up until the start of the Second World War. It

Fun Facts

Looking for the perfect cat to match the décor of your house? With over 300 variations of coat and colour, the veritable Dulux catalogue that is the Oriental Shorthair could make it the ideal breed for you!

was only in the 1950s that work on resurrecting and developing the breed commenced in earnest. With the "non-Siamese" type now being referred to as the "Foreign", different coloured types started to appear – some of these such as the Korat and the Havana taking on

new names of their own.

Just like its Siamese cousin, the Oriental Shorthair is an intelligent and companionable cat. With an inquisitive nature, they enjoy playing games of fetch, and love to express their pleasure with an attention grabbing vocal display.

Persian Longhair

The Persian Longhair, with its silky coat and distinctive turned up nose, is thought to have originated in Turkey and Persia before arriving in Europe in the early part of the seventeenth century via Italy. The Venetian traveller and writer Pietro della Valle (1586 – 1652) is generally credited with their introduction having spent 12 years from 1614 on a cultural pilgrimage to Asia Minor. Della Valle described his extensive adventures in a series of 54 letters that were later published in three

Fun Facts

After three years on the run, having fled from his native Italy to Canada in an attempt to escape the long arm of the law, Mafia member Marco Milano agreed to return for trial on the condition that he could share his cell with his beloved Persian. Milano and Minu the cat are currently serving an eight-year sentence.

volumes between 1650 and 1653. In one, he wrote of a very tame species of cat from the northeast Persian province of Khorasan whose "beauty consists in the colour of their hair, which is grey… shining, soft as silk". He went on to describe that he had collected "four couple" of these felines which he intended to bring with him on his return to Italy.

In later years, other grand tourists brought examples of this striking longhair back to France and then on to British shores where they inappropriately became known as French Cats until the mid-nineteenth century and the establishment of the first cat fancies. From this time, the simple term Longhair was instead used to describe not only the Persian but also the Angora with both breeds being judged together; only in the early twentieth century with the inauguration of the GCCF were the two breeds finally separated.

The Persian is a cool, calm and collected breed disinclined to take part in any activity it might consider to be close to hard work. They are gentle and affectionate and, whilst they are more than content to be curled up aside or

Persian Longhair	
Place of Origin	Persia and Turkey
Date of Origin	1600s
Other Names	None
Weight	3.5 – 7kg
Lifespan	> 15 years
Temperament	Calm and affectionate

on top of their human companions, they are just as content to be left to their own devices.

Ragdoll

The curious Ragdoll is truly unique amongst cats. With its strong Birman-like physique and purposeful gait, see one trotting before you and you could easily be forgiven for imagining that it is just another Longhair happily going about its daily routine. The difference, however, becomes apparent the very moment you pick it up when it will automatically relax all of its muscles to become totally limp and floppy – just like the toy ragdoll it is named after.

The breed was first discovered by a somewhat controversial woman by the name of Ann Baker of the Raggedy Ann cattery in Riverside, California. She mated her white Persian-Angora type cat, Josephine, with a Burmese type belonging to her neighbour. The resulting kittens displayed this remarkable limp nature. The true cause of this phenomenon remains unclear, however Ann Baker, a colourful character with a somewhat abstract outlook on life, claimed that it was all to do with a road accident in which Josephine had been involved and how evil government geneticists had subsequently altered her DNA whilst she was undergoing treatment. This brush with the fabled Men in Black seems as likely as her later assertions that the Ragdoll cat represented a link between humans and alien life forms.

Fortunately for potential owners, the Ragdoll has not inherited any of the more bizarre traits of its original breeder. It is, in fact, one of the most relaxed and laid back of all the domestic breeds being undemanding, tolerant and extremely gentle. They are an excellent choice as a household pet and, due to their flaccid nature, prove very popular with young children who just love to pick them up.

Ragdoll	
Place of Origin	United States
Date of Origin	1960s
Other Names	RagaMuffin
Weight	4.5 – 9kg
Lifespan	10 – 12 years
Temperament	Laid back and gentle

Fun Facts

Socks and Cookie the cats on the popular children's BBC television programme Blue Peter are both Ragdolls. Socks joined the programme in January 2007 whilst Cookie made his debut later in the same year.

LITTLE BOOK OF **CATS**   **101**

Russian Blue

Russian Blue	
Place of Origin	Russia
Date of Origin	Pre 1800s
Other Names	Archangel Cat, Russian Shorthair, Foreign Blue
Weight	3 – 5.5kg
Lifespan	17 – 19 years
Temperament	Shy and sensitive

With piercing emerald-green eyes and a regal air, the Russian Blue is a natural breed of cat and not the engineered result of a selective breeding programme. Known first as the Archangel Cat, having originated from the north Russian seaport of the same name, it arrived in Great Britain and Northern Europe aboard trading ships in the 1860s before first being shown to the public at the 1875 Crystal Palace show. Despite a lack of Iberian or Mediterranean connections, it has also been referred to as the Spanish Cat or the Maltese; a name which persisted in the United States for many years.

The breed suffered badly during the Second World War and subsequent attempts to revive its fortunes using

British Blue and Siamese outcrosses almost led to its complete disappearance – the resulting kittens instead resembling Blue Siamese. Only a concerted effort in the late 1960s by dedicated breeders on both sides of the Atlantic guaranteed its survival and a welcome return to the original type.

The Russian Blue is an immensely loyal breed. It is, nevertheless, quiet and sensitive and shows a tendency to be rather shy and reserved around strangers or uncommon surroundings. Once happy in its environment it will, however, blossom and put on a display of running, jumping and climbing to rival any other breed you could care to mention.

Scottish Fold

Scottish Fold	
Place of Origin	Scotland
Date of Origin	1961
Other Names	Highland Fold
Weight	2.4 – 6.9kg
Lifespan	12 – 14 years
Temperament	Gentle and companionable

The Scottish Fold is an unusual breed in that it is the subject of a natural mutation that causes a fold in its ear cartilage. Evidence of cats with folded ears has existed for well over 200 years however, the Scottish Fold breed as we now recognise it, can be traced back to a humble white cat named Susie who was born on a farm near Coupar Angus, Scotland in 1961. Her folded ears caused people to remark that she had the appearance of a small white owl. Although the breed was

originally registered with the GCCF in the late 1960s, approval was later withdrawn after claims that the breed suffered from inner ear infections and deafness. This stance is still maintained although many avid breeders of the type vehemently contest these findings. The breed is, however, recognised by the ACA, CFA and TICA and can regularly be seen at shows across the United States where it remains a rare but popular attraction.

Folds are gentle in temperament and mix well with other animals, with their farmyard ancestry showing through in their surprisingly hardy nature. They adore any form of human companionship and love to play games but expect this to be a mutually appreciated activity.

Fun Facts

Before receiving the name by which we know them today, Scottish Folds were known as Lop-Eared Cats.

Selkirk Rex

Selkirk Rex	
Place of Origin	United States
Date of Origin	1987
Other Names	None
Weight	3 – 5kg
Lifespan	> 15 years
Temperament	Gentle and reserved

In contrast to its fine-boned, svelte Devon and Cornish Rex genetic cousins, the American born Selkirk Rex is a heavily-boned medium to large cat with a surprising weight. The very first Selkirk was a quirky little blue, cream and white kitten named Miss DePesto of NoFace, "Pest" for short, who was born at the "For Pet's Sake" animal shelter in Sheridan, Montana during 1987. After several unsuccessful homings, she came into the possession of Livingston resident Jeri Montana, a breeder of Longhairs, after a friend at the local Bozeman Humane Society brought the cat to her attention.

She was soon mated to Photo Finish

Fun Facts

Jeri Newman originally claimed that the Selkirk Rex was named after a mountain range in Wyoming close to the town where Miss DePesto was born. When it was pointed out that the Selkirk Mountains were, in fact, located in Idaho and British Columbia she admitted that she had really named the breed after a family member!

of Deekay, a champion black Persian, resulting in the birth, on 4 July 1988, of a litter of six kittens both long and shorthair – three of which bore Pest's trademark wavy coat. Recognised in the United States by TICA in 1992 and the CFA in 2000, the first Selkirk Rex cats arrived in the United Kingdom in 2002 where the breed is awaiting affiliation to the GCCF.

Like Miss DePesto herself, the Selkirk Rex is a relaxed, laid back and gentle breed. They are affectionate by nature and enjoy human company – especially if it involves a good cuddle. A true colour swatch cat, the Selkirk can be seen in all colours and patterns including pointed, smoke and mink.

Siamese

One of the most popular and easily recognisable of all the cat breeds, the elegant Siamese can trace its origins back to Thailand and the revered Royal Court of Siam. Seen in the pages of the much lauded Cat Book Poems created at some point between 1358 and 1767 during the Ayudha period of Thai history, the breed was often regarded as sacred and was used as a guard at Buddhist temples. A symbol of good luck, to be presented with a Siamese kitten was seen to be a great honour. However, if you were unlucky enough to be caught stealing one from the Royal Court your fortune would be less promising; the crime was

punishable by instant death!

Siamese finally arrived in Britain during the mid-nineteenth century with an example being seen at the Crystal Palace show for the first time in 1871. It would seem that, at this time, the breed was not received with quite the same level of appreciation it enjoys today as this pioneering feline was described to be a "nightmare" cat that was "ugly and frightening"!

In more recent times there has been a tendency to breed a more slender, fine- boned Siamese. Whilst these are often favoured in showing circles, there remains a devout and enthusiastic band of breeders and owners who still favour the slightly heavier traditional Siamese.

If there is one attribute for which the Siamese is most known it must surely be its vocal ability. If you are looking for a peaceful and introverted feline then look elsewhere! They are a gregarious and extrovert breed by nature and love to be kept busy. Siamese do not take well to being left alone but are, however, more than happy to share their time with other cats.

Siamese	
Place of Origin	Thailand
Date of Origin	1600s
Other Names	Royal Cat of Siam
Weight	2.5 – 5.5kg
Lifespan	15 – 17 years
Temperament	Extrovert and highly vocal

Siberian

Although the Siberian cat has only recently become recognised as a pedigree breed, its origins can be traced back as far as the thirteenth century where they are said to have walked alongside monks patrolling the high walls of ancient monasteries. However, with pet ownership restricted under the communist regime that controlled the Soviet states from 1917, it was not until the late 1980s that the breed came to the attention of the showing fraternity.

The first was shown in the city of Leningrad (now St Petersburg) in March 1987 with the official breed standard being constructed the following year by breeders Olga Mironova and Olga Frolova. After 13 of the breed were exhibited at a Moscow show in 1989 the newly formed Soviet Felinology Federation registered the Siberian under Certificate No 1. Siberians were first introduced to Europe and the United States in the 1990s but did not find their way to British shores until 2002 when the first examples were imported from the United States.

One of the largest domestic breeds, Siberians are playful, affectionate and loyal by nature and can become highly attached to their owners, choosing to follow their every move if at all possible. Often described as dog-like in their personality, it is not unknown for them to enjoy walks on a harness, swimming and even going for car journeys.

Siberian	
Place of Origin	Russia
Date of Origin	1200s
Other Names	Siberian Forest Cat
Weight	4.5 – 9kg
Lifespan	12 – 15 years
Temperament	Loyal and dog-like

Singapura

Officially classed as the world's smallest breed of cat, the delicate Singapura's ancestors are reputed to have inhabited the open drains and sewers on the island of Singapore for at least 300 years. It is thought to have originated from countless felines that arrived in the busy Asiatic port aboard ships from across the globe.

Controversy surrounded the registering of the Singapura when it was revealed that the three foundation cats of the pedigree breed were not plucked straight from the drains of Singapore as originally claimed but had, in fact been bred in the United States before being temporarily exported to the Far East and then re-imported. After a lengthy investigation, however, the breed's credibility was reinstated when it was disclosed that the felines in question were direct descendents of four legitimate Singapore cats that had been privately imported several years earlier.

The Singapura loves human company preferring the warmth of a lap or the elevation of a willing shoulder to a solitary cushion or basket. In fact, given the opportunity, they will always seek out a high vantage point and if one should go missing, the best place to start looking is invariably the top of wardrobes, curtain rails or open beams. They love and crave attention and retain a kitten-like curiosity and playful nature throughout their lives.

Singapura	
Place of Origin	Singapore
Date of Origin	1975
Other Names	River Cat, Singapore Drain Cat
Weight	2 – 4kg
Lifespan	14 years
Temperament	Lively and devoted

Snowshoe

Snowshoe	
Place of Origin	United States
Date of Origin	1960s
Other Names	None
Weight	2.5 – 5.5kg
Lifespan	12 years
Temperament	Friendly and outgoing

Considered a rare breed, the charismatic Snowshoe breed was created in the 1960s by Philadelphia based breeder Dorothy Hinds-Daugherty after she began to cross her Siamese with bi-colour American Shorthairs. The resulting kittens combined the dramatic pointing of the much loved Siamese with frosty white socks on each foot, earning them the name of Snowshoe and the occasional nickname of Silver Laces.

There are two varieties of the breed: the classic mitted Snowshoe which, in addition to its white paws may also display white markings on its face, and the bi-colour which is easily recognisable by the inverted V of white on its face. Lean and muscular, the breed is often said to have the appearance of a runner rather than that of a weightlifter.

Snowshoes go out of their way

Fun Facts

It can take two years for a Snowshoe to gain its full coat colour – they are all born white and darken over time.

to be friendly towards all members of the family and like to show their appreciation with a melodic display of their vocal capabilities. They are sweet natured and affectionate, thoroughly enjoy playing energetic games whenever the opportunity arises but do, however, require a great deal of care and attention and consequently cannot be left alone for long periods of time.

Somali

Somali	
Place of Origin	North American
Date of Origin	1963
Other Names	Longhaired Abyssinian
Weight	3.5 – 5.5kg
Lifespan	12 – 14 years
Temperament	Intelligent and good natured

The wonderfully wild-looking Somali is a longhaired version of the Abyssinian – its rich coat carrying as many as 10 bands of colour to give it a truly unique appearance. The longhaired gene is thought to have been introduced into the Abyssinian gene pool at some point during the 1930s with one of the first known carriers being the delightfully named Mrs Mew – a hybrid Abyssinian wartime stray who was found during the London Blitz in 1940.

Although longhaired Abyssinians were first shown in the United States in the mid-1950s, it was not until the 1960s that the potential of this breed started to be taken seriously. In 1963 a longhaired Aby was entered as a joke into the Abyssinian class at the Calgary Show. Whilst its presence caused a great deal of amusement from other breeders, it also managed to catch the eye of CCA Judge Ken McGill who, charmed by its beautiful appearance, asked its owner, Mary Mailing, for one to breed and subsequently set up what has become one of the oldest Somali lines in existence.

Many traditional Abyssinian breeders did not want to see the introduction of a longhaired version of their beloved feline but the efforts of a few dedicated

advocates bore fruit with the foundation of the Somali Cat Club in 1972. The breed was subsequently accepted by the FIFe in 1982 and the GCCF in 1991.

Like their Aby relations, Somalis are highly intelligent and good natured. They thoroughly enjoy human company and love toys and playing games, but tend to be a little shy from time to time. They enjoy outdoor life but are prone to wander, so a secure garden is an absolute must.

Fun Facts

Not wanting to ignore the breed's heritage, one of the Somali's early campaigners, Evelyn Mague, named the breed after Somalia - the African nation that borders Ethiopia, the country previously known as Abyssinia.

Sphynx

There are big cats, tiny cats, athletic cats and lazy cats. If, however, there is one type of cat that is guaranteed to grab the attention it must surely be the Sphynx – the birthday suit cat!

The first properly recorded hairless breed was the Mexican Hairless. Now extinct, it is known that a couple from New Mexico received a pair from local Pueblo Indians in 1902 who claimed that they were the last survivors of an ancient breed of cat kept by the Aztecs. Sadly this type was lost over the years through the lack of an established breeding programme.

Although several hairless kittens were discovered in Toronto in 1963,

it was not until 1966 that the first true breeding programme was initiated when a domestic shorthair unexpectedly produced a hairless kitten of its own. These early cats were known initially as the Canadian Hairless, then the Moonstone and Canadian Sphynx before it became a recognised breed as the Sphynx in the mid-1970s.

Whilst clearly not to everybody's aesthetic taste, the Sphynx is a surprisingly affectionate and outgoing cat that loves to be picked up and cuddled – the lack of a thick insulating outer coat making it surprisingly warm to the touch. A highly talkative breed, it is said to be a champion purrer – a pastime that often accompanies its characteristic pose of standing with one foreleg raised.

Sphynx	
Place of Origin	Canada
Date of Origin	1966
Other Names	Canadian Hairless
Weight	3.5 – 7kg
Lifespan	14 years
Temperament	Affectionate and chatty

Tonkinese

Tonkinese	
Place of Origin	United States
Date of Origin	1950s
Other Names	Golden Siamese
Weight	2.5 – 5.5kg
Lifespan	17 – 19 years
Temperament	Affectionate and inquisitive

A lthough its exotic name would have you believe that the lovely Tonkinese bears Asiatic origins it is actually a product of the United States. But even this undisputable fact bears a curious twist to its long elegant tail. It is thought that Tonkinese may have initially been imported to the United Kingdom in the nineteenth century as Chocolate Siamese although the first documented Tonk seen in the West was most certainly Wong Mau: a naturally bred Siamese-Burmese hybrid born in Rangoon who was imported into the United States and formed the basis of the Burmese, an altogether different breed.

The foundation of the modern breed as we know it commenced in the 1950s and was the result of an intentional crossing of a Siamese and a Burmese by American breeder Millar Greer to produce what was originally known

Fun Facts

Although the breed is now known and recognised as the Tonkinese, it was first dubbed the Tonkanese.

as a Golden Siamese. For a decade the breed remained largely ignored until it reappeared amongst the cat fancy under the new name of Tonkinese – the result of parallel breeding programmes by Canadian breeder Margaret Conroy and American breeder Jane Barletta. The breed was officially recognised in Canada in 1965 and then in the United States seven years later. It would take an additional 20 years for the Tonkinese to gain acceptance by the British GCCF.

Tonks are amongst the most affectionate of all breeds. Highly people-orientated, they will do their level best to be part of your activities about the house, accompanying your every move and sometimes letting their inquisitive nature get in the way of their survival instincts. They are easily trained, love being set tasks and will happily chat away to you all day long.

Turkish Van

Turkish Van	
Place of Origin	Turkey
Date of Origin	Pre 1800s
Other Names	Turkish Swimming Cat
Weight	3 – 8.5kg
Lifespan	12 – 14 years
Temperament	Intelligent and aqautic

An avid swimmer, the attractive Turkish Van seems to be a contradiction of all we have come to recognise in natural feline behaviour. Whilst other breeds would shudder at the thought of even venturing out in a light shower, the Van is minded to think that there is nothing better than an early morning dip.

The breed originates from the Van Province in the far east of Turkey just touching the Iranian border. There exists a great lake which, over the centuries, appears to have acted as the cat's

personal playground. The Turkish Van was first introduced into the West in the 1950s when Laura Lushington and Sonia Halliday were presented with a pair by a hotel manager whilst visiting the country. On returning home, the cats bred and, with three identical auburn and white kittens on her hands, Miss Lushington realised that she had been given something special. In order to provide the necessary dual breeding line, she went back to Turkey to acquire another pair and set to establishing a breeding programme that ultimately gave us the pedigree breed we know today.

The Turkish Van is an extremely intelligent breed of cat with a soft voice and a demeanour to match. They make excellent companions and are more than happy living alongside other felines. It must always be remembered that they enjoy their watersports and they will thoroughly appreciate a swim in the bath should no pool be available.

Fun Facts

The Turkish Van is a truly adaptable breed – it has to be! In the summer months the temperatures in the east of Turkey can easily reach 40C whilst in the winter they can drop as low as -35C.

ALSO AVAILABLE IN THE LITTLE BOOK SERIES

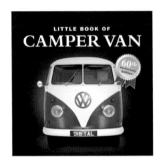
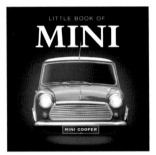

ALSO AVAILABLE IN THE LITTLE BOOK SERIES

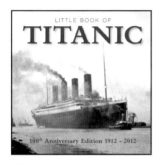

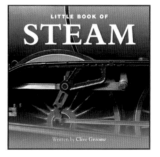

The pictures in this book were provided courtesy of the following:

GETTY IMAGES
www.gettyimages.co.uk

SHUTTERSTOCK
www.shutterstock.com

CATWORLD MAGAZINE
www.catworld.co.uk

Design and artwork by Scott Giarnese

Published by G2 Entertainment Limited

Publishers Jules Gammond and Edward Adams

Written by Jon Stroud